WHAT IS MY NAME?

Epic Whizz Inc. publishing

written by Marie-anne M. K. jung

illustrated and written by sebastian j. H. jung

Chul-Su was sitting on a bench in the playground watching children play soccer.

He wanted to play with them, but he was afraid to tell them because he couldn't speak English well.

So, he came back home with a sad face.

"Chul-Su, did you have a good day at school?" Dad asked.

Chul-Su said, "I was just watching. There were many children playing soccer.

I wanted to play with them but didn't know how to say it in English.

But I saw that their soccer ball was old and didn't roll well."

Dad smiled and said, "How about asking them to play with you tomorrow?

They may not know you want to play with them if you don't tell them."

Chul-Su wondered, "Can I?"

The next day, Dad bought him a shiny, brand-new soccer ball.

And Dad said, "Are you ready to play soccer with your friends?"

But Chul-Su, who did not have the confidence to speak to them,

was sitting on the bench again.

He was just hugging his shiny soccer ball while watching other

children play soccer with an old ball.

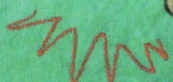

Then, suddenly, the old soccer ball rolled toward Chul-Su.

A boy approached Chul-Su to grab the ball, and he noticed the shiny soccer ball in Chul-Su's arms.

"Hi, I'm Fabien. You have an awesome soccer ball!

Hey, you guys, come on up here! Here is a new player

with a cool soccer ball!"

Then, all the children who were playing soccer gathered

in front of Chul-Su.

"What's going on?"

"A new player?"

"Look! He has an awesome soccer ball!"

"We don't have enough players yet. Do you want to join us?"

Chul-Su didn't understand the children's words,

but he got brave and told them:

"This is 축구공 /chuggugong/! /chuggugong/."

Chul-Su said it in Korean.

"Oh, you call this /chuggugong/? I call it un ballon de football." Fabien said.

He can speak French.

"I call it balón de fútbol!" Zita said.

She can speak Spanish.

"I call it ФУТБОЛЬНИЙ М'ЯЧ/*futbol'nyy m'yach*/!" Maxym said.

He can speak Ukrainian.

"I call it サッカーボール/*sakkābōru*/!" Yoshida said.

He can speak Japanese.

"I call it كرة القدم /kurat alqadam/!" Muhammad said.

He can speak Arabic.

"Anyway, we call it a soccer ball!"

"Let's play together, new player!"

"Hey! My friend, kick the ball to me!" Fabien said.

Chul-Su kicked the ball powerfully into the playground.

The End

A soccer ball

Un ballon de football

축구공

balón de fútbol

футбольний м'яч

サッカーボール

كرة القدم

Authors' Note

This picture book uses soccer balls as real-life examples to convey the importance of understanding and respecting diversity from a child's perspective.

Through colourful, aesthetic watercolor illustrations and rhythmic reading with repeated rhymes, we help children develop a sense of enjoyment from reading as well as an inclusive, open, and respectful mind toward other languages and cultures. In addition, through activities to find a common ground using various objects and cultures around them, these children can naturally take pride in their own language and culture as well as learn respect for other languages and cultures.

As people who have immigrated to Canada, we have seen a lot of children who have emigrated to English-speaking countries. Children living in English-speaking countries sometimes reject a new immigrant child if he or she does not speak English well—without even understanding why. On the other hand, immigrant children may be ashamed of their inability to speak English well, or they may be embarrassed to or even refuse to use their native language.

So, this picture book—through the appearance of Cheol-Su, a new immigrant child, and his new soccer ball—conveys through beautiful sounds that everything has different names in different languages and that these differences are not something to be ashamed of but rather are special. In addition, the book shows, from the pure perspective of a child, that despite differing languages and cultures, all children can be united through one medium, like a soccer ball.

We humans belong to one community with the same destiny, living on one planet—Earth. Various countries, peoples, languages, and cultures coexist in this world. Countries such as Canada and the United States that were created by immigrants can be seen as countries that have moved the world. Citizens of these immigrant countries communicate with one another through English, but they also have their own cultures, traditions, and languages that they use in their homes. We want children to recognize and acknowledge this from an early age to prevent discrimination in society based on race, culture, language, or any other reason.

Epic
Whizz Inc.™
publishing

Published by Epic Whizz Inc.
First Edition, 2024
ISBN: 978-1-989748-50-3
ISBN: 978-1-989748-49-7 (eBook)
www.epicwhizz.com
www.animahero.com

www.ingramcontent.com/pod-product-compliance
Lightning Source LLC
Chambersburg PA
CBHW061354090426
42739CB00002B/28